Chris Mullin

by Mark Stewart

ACKNOWLEDGMENTS
The editors wish to thank Chris Mullin for his cooperation in preparing this book.
Thanks also to Integrated Sports International for their assistance.

PHOTO CREDITS
All photos courtesy AP/Wide World Photos, Inc. except the following:

Rich Kane/Sports Chrome – Cover
Golden State Warriors – 23 top right, 32, 41, 45
The Chris Mullin Fund – 4 top left, 43
Mark Stewart – 48

STAFF
Project Coordinator: John Sammis, Cronopio Publishing
Series Design Concept: The Sloan Group
Design and Electronic Page Makeup: Jaffe Enterprises, and
        Digital Communications Services, Inc.

LIBRARY OF CONGRESS CATALOGING-IN-PUBLICATION DATA
Stewart, Mark.
    Chris Mullin / by Mark Stewart.
      p. cm. – (Grolier all-pro biographies)
    Includes index.
    Summary: A brief biography of the All-Star point guard for the Golden State Warriors.
    ISBN 0-516-20166-2 (lib. binding) – ISBN 0-516-26015-4 (pbk.)
    Mullin, Chris, 1963-   – Juvenile literature. 2. Basketball players—United States—
Juvenile literature. [1. Mullin, Chris, 1963-   . 2. Basketball players.]
    I. Title. II. Series.
    GV884.M85S82 1996
    796.323'092—dc20
    [B]   96-14049
                                                                              CIP
                                                                               AC

Grolier **ALL-PRO** *Biographies*™

Chris

Mullin

by

Mark Stewart

CHILDREN'S PRESS®
A Division of Grolier Publishing
New York • London • Hong Kong • Sydney
Danbury, Connecticut

Contents

Who

Am I?

It's not the end of the world if you have a problem. It's what you do with it—how you adjust to it and deal with it—that counts. Looking cool and acting like everything's okay is not the answer. I should know. I had a problem, and I was afraid to ask for help. It almost ruined my life, but I worked on my problem and survived. My name is Chris Mullin, and this is my story . . . "

"I had a problem, and I was afraid to ask for help."

Growing Up

The schoolyards of Brooklyn, New York, have been turning out tough, talented basketball players for as long as anyone can remember. Chris Mullin grew up in this basketball-crazy atmosphere, and he was as crazy about basketball as anyone. Starting in elementary school, he would spend hours each day working on his shooting and ballhandling.

By the time Chris was nine years old, all of that practice was beginning to show. He entered a national foul-shooting contest and did so well that he reached the finals in Kansas City, Missouri. He made 23 of 25 shots to win the championship.

When Chris was 12, he attended a summer camp for young basketball players run by a man named Lou Carnesecca. Carnesecca coached the team at St. John's University, which

was in the borough of Queens, just a few miles from Chris's home. Carnesecca liked what he saw in Chris, and Chris liked Carnesecca. They did not know it then, but many years later, they would help each other to reach the NCAA Final Four.

Chris's father, Rod Mullin was a customs inspector at Kennedy Airport in New York. His job was to check packages and luggage that arrived on airplanes coming from outside of the United States. He often worked 16-hour days to put food on the table for Chris and his three brothers and sister. Chris's mother, Eileen, worked for the phone company before her children were born. After that, she had all she could handle keeping the Mullin house running smoothly.

Rod Mullin was very happy that Chris was becoming a good basketball player. Back

in the 1950s, Rod had been one of Brooklyn's top basketball stars, playing with future pros such as Doug Moe, Larry Brown, Connie Hawkins, and Billy Cunningham. As important as basketball was in the Mullin

Chris's father played against basketball greats Doug Moe (left) and Connie Hawkins (right).

house, however, education was the top priority. School first and sports second—that was the rule.

Chris liked school a lot. He lived just 80 steps from the entrance of St. Thomas Aquinas. His favorite subject was history, his favorite class was gym, and his favorite teacher was Sister Mary Romuel. She taught Chris in fourth grade, and they got along very well. One thing Chris did not like at first was math. Sometimes he just could not get the answer to a homework problem. He would have to wait until after dinner to get help from his parents—and that meant he could not go out and play. Chris began to improve when he realized that he was already using math whenever he calculated the statistics of his favorite player, John Havlicek.

Outside of school, Chris read everything he could find on his favorite athletes. "Reading is the most important thing you can learn," Chris says. "Unless you know an adult who is unable to read, you cannot imagine how horrible life is without this basic skill. I know that sometimes kids 'slip through the cracks' and get pushed along through school without ever learning how to read. Well, you don't have to be that kid. If you feel that you are having difficulty reading, tell someone about it. Believe me, I know how tough it can be to admit you have a problem, and it is embarrassing to ask for help. But it won't get any easier if you wait. The thing to do is reach out. Now. There are people in your school who will be there for you. That's what teaching is all about."

When it was time to choose a high school, Chris told his parents he would like to go to Power Memorial in Manhattan. His older brother, Roddy, was already enrolled there and playing on the basketball team. Power was glad to have Chris, who could already shoot as well as any of the older boys on the team. Chris led the freshman and junior-varsity teams to city championships, but he was not happy. He missed his friends back in Brooklyn, and he did not get along with his coach.

A few weeks after his sophomore year began, Chris made a big decision. He was going to leave Power and transfer to Xavieran High School, which was closer to his house. School rules said that transfer students had to sit out a full school year of athletics, so Chris would not be able to play basketball until he was a senior. Would college recruiters forget about him? It was a big gamble, but Chris decided that his own happiness was worth it.

During his sophomore and junior years, Chris trained like a boxer preparing for a championship fight. He knew he would have just one year to reestablish himself as a top player, and he wanted to make sure he was ready. After school and on weekends, Chris went looking for the best games on the playgrounds of New York City. Sometimes, this meant traveling by subway into very tough neighborhoods. He was scared at first, but once he got into the flow of the games, he forgot all about the danger and simply did what he did best: score and play defense. In the evenings, he shot hoops at his old elementary school. The night janitor knew Chris and gave him a spare key to the gym. Chris also got plenty of practice against his brothers in the family driveway—these were the roughest games of all!

When Chris was allowed to play again, he was definitely ready. In his first game for Xavieran, he poured in 38 points in front of a standing-room-only crowd. A few months later, Xavieran won the state championship. When college recruiters started calling, Chris listened to their offers and discussed his options with his mother and father. The more Chris thought about it, the more he wanted to go to a school that was close to home. The closest college with a good basketball team was St. John's University, where his old friend Lou

Lou Carnesecca was head coach at St. John's University.

Carnesecca was still coaching. When Chris announced he would attend St. John's, many experts were surprised. They expected him to attend a school such as UCLA or North Carolina—big-name universities with big-time basketball programs. But Chris could see that St. John's was a school on the rise. And the newly formed Big East Conference was one of the most competitive in the country. Once again, he was confident that he had made the right choice.

Life was pretty good for Chris during the spring and summer of 1981. He seemed to have everything a teenager could ask

Chris chose to stay close to home and attend St. John's University.

for. Once in a while, he celebrated by drinking a few beers. No one thought too much about it—not even his father, who had quit drinking the year before. Certainly, no one suspected that alcohol would nearly destroy his basketball career.

College

T he St. John's campus was just 20 minutes from Chris Mullin's home. Everything he knew and loved was close by, and that helped him do what Coach Carnesecca wanted his players to do most: focus on basketball. When Chris was not attending class, he practically lived in the gym. In fact, during a 1982 blizzard, he and his friend Larry Falabella spent the entire weekend stranded inside Alumni Hall. They played one-on-one and H-O-R-S-E all day, and slept in Coach Carnesecca's office at night!

Chris had a brilliant freshman season. He finished second on the St. John's Redmen in scoring and assists, and his 43 steals were the most of any St. John's player. He was even better as a sophomore, winning the Big East Player of the Year and Big East Tournament MVP awards. Chris also got his first taste of international basketball when he made the U.S. national team that played in the 1983 Pan Am Games.

hris teamed with Big East stars Willie Glass and Walter Berry to begin the 1984–85 season with a 14–1 record. That was good enough to give St. John's a number-one national ranking.

Chris truly came into his own as a senior. His passing and defensive skills blossomed, and he sometimes seemed able to score at will. In the 1985 NCAA Tournament, Chris led the Redmen to the Final Four by averaging more than 25 points per game. It took a team effort by Big East rival Georgetown to shut Chris down in the national semifinal, but he still ended up leading all tournament scorers with 110 points.

As a senior, Chris became the Big East Conference all-time leading scorer.

Years

Chris just kept getting better. In his third season for St. John's, he became the Big East's all-time leading scorer and earned All-America honors. That summer, Chris competed in the Olympics as a member of the U.S. basketball team. He scored 93 points in eight games to help future NBA stars Michael Jordan, Patrick Ewing, Wayman Tisdale, and Alvin Robertson win the gold medal.

As a freshman, Chris (left) was St. John's second-highest scorer.

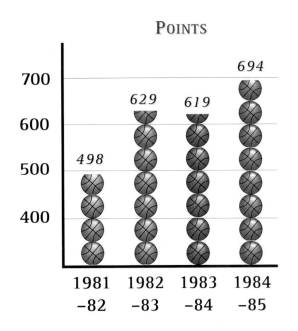

POINTS

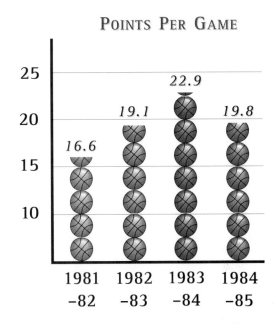

POINTS PER GAME

Although the Redmen failed to win the NCAA Tournament, their 31-4 record that year is still the best in school history.

After the 1984–85 season, Chris was voted College Player of the Year. The award did not mean that Chris was the only important man on his team. "One of the key things I learned in school was—whether I was part of a team or part of a class—how important it is to be part of a group. I learned that putting yourself first doesn't always make sense. Sometimes, it's to your advantage to do what's best for the group."

The Story

As the 1985 NBA draft approached, Chris Mullin hoped that he could stay in New York and play for the Knicks. When the Knicks were awarded the first pick in the lottery, however, Chris knew he would be heading elsewhere. Patrick Ewing was everyone's first choice that spring, and the Knicks announced right away that they would select the Georgetown center on draft day. When that day came, Chris was selected by the Golden State Warriors, who play in Oakland, California.

Chris was completely unprepared for life as a professional basketball player. It took several months for him and the Warriors to agree on the details of his contract. He missed all of training camp, plus the first six games of the season. When Chris finally joined the team, he

Even though he wanted to play in New York, Chris was happy to be drafted by Golden State.

Continues

found a very different situation than he had expected. The Warriors had told him all along that they needed a leader who could set an example for the rest of the team. But whenever Chris tried to put a spark into the Warriors, other players told him to cut it out. They did not like it when the rookie urged them to play as a team, and when Chris stayed late after practice for extra shooting, he was told that he was making them look bad. Sometimes he wondered if they really wanted to win at all!

As a rookie, Chris gave it everything he had.

With no friends and nothing to do, Chris spent a lot of time by himself. He found that he felt better after having a few beers. After a few drinks, he could hardly remember what was bothering him. And after a few more, he passed out and went to sleep. His drinking was becoming a big problem, and it began to affect his play.

As the Warriors continued to lose—and Chris continued to drink—it became more and more difficult for him to play the game he loved. In fact, he remembers days when he did not care if he ever played basketball again. A few weeks into the 1987-88 season, Chris missed two practices and was suspended from the team. Coach Don Nelson demanded that his star player get some help. So Chris checked into Centinela Hospital in Los Angeles for a 30-day rehabilitation program. He did not take it very seriously at first, but soon he came to view his drinking as a sickness. If he had a lung disease, would he smoke cigarettes? No, he thought, of course not. That made it easier to stop drinking, although it is never easy to stop forever. Chris knows he must fight his addiction every day.

When Chris returned to the Warriors, he began to realize how stupid he had been. He rededicated himself to hard work and practice, and the results were incredible. He became one of the NBA's top scorers, averaging more than 25 points per game five years in a row. His steals and assist totals also improved, and he now is considered a complete player.

"Although I'm known best for my shooting, I get more satisfaction from passing to an open teammate. To me, there's nothing like playing unselfishly—whether you're at the end of a play or the beginning of a play. When you 'click' with your teammates that's a really satisfying thing."

Chris has yet to win an NBA championship, but that is not as important to him as it might have been 10 years ago. He has already won a far more important victory. Chris won back his own life.

An accurate hook shot helped Chris average over 25 points a game in five straight seasons (1988–93).

Timeline

**1985:
Named
College
Player of
the Year**

**1981:
Enrolls at
St. John's
University**

**1985:
Joins NBA
Golden
State
Warriors**

1993: Averages over 25 points per game for fifth straight year

1989: Scores career-high 47 points in a game against the Los Angeles Clippers

1995: Makes career-best 45.2% of his three-point attempts

Game

Chris and teammate Walter Berry are the only consensus All-Americans to play for St. John's since World War II.

Chris is known for being quick on his feet. "I especially like fooling people, faking out the other guy."

Chris has worn seven different uniform numbers since elementary school. When he got to the NBA, he chose 17 in honor of his favorite player, Hall of Famer John Havlicek, and because St. Patrick's Day falls on March 17.

Action!

This life wasn't just given to me—I worked to get it. I've been on the other side of the fence and I like this side better."

Chris is one of the best free-throw shooters in NBA history. Shooting accurately demands hours of practice. "Everybody else is working hard, so I better go a little more."

Chris and Michael Jordan were reunited in 1992 on the Dream Team. They won their first Olympic gold medal together in 1984.

Magic Johnson and Chris enjoy a moment during a timeout. Chris says, "I have fun every moment I'm on the court."

Win or lose, Chris thinks of his teammates as family. "The thing I like best about basketball is the sharing you do with your teammates . . . it's just like a family situation."

Chris and Tim Hardaway (with ball) were named Warriors co-captains in 1990.

Chris knows that he has to play physically and endure injuries to be a top player. "In the NBA, you do almost anything to win."

Dealing

he first step Chris had to take in overcoming his drinking problem was to admit he had a problem. That was not easy. After all, he was a professional basketball player. But after spending a few weeks in a rehabilitation program with alcohol and drug addicts, he began to see that in many ways he was no different than they were.

Chris reflects on his struggle with alcohol: "I was trying to be a great drinker and a great basketball player, and I found out that I couldn't do both. I gave up one and now I'm pretty good at the other."

With It

Back from the hospital, Chris struggles through his first practice.

How Does

He Do It?

hris Mullin's training schedule is rough, even by NBA standards. During a typical off-day, he works out on a stair-climber, rides a stationary bicycle, and lifts weights. Then it is off to the gym, where Chris practices three-pointers for an hour, then takes 200 foul shots.

Why does he work out so hard? Not just to improve at basketball, but because he loves it! "I feel bad for people who struggle to get up and go to work. I get up *early* to get over to the gym."

Because he practices so hard, Chris has to soak his feet in ice water after every workout.

Family

Chris and Liz Mullin have two children, Sean and Christopher. Whenever Chris is in the New York area to play the Knicks or the New Jersey Nets, he tries to get the rest of the family together for a big party. His three brothers are all involved in basketball, and his sister is a nurse. Sadly, Chris's mother and father both died of cancer. His father's death in 1990 was especially difficult because, as recovering alcoholics, they had developed a very special relationship after Chris completed his rehab in 1988. "Family is the most important thing in your life. That's how I was raised."

Chris's parents, Eileen and Rod, were all smiles after Chris signed a contract with Golden State.

Matters

Say What?

Here's what basketball people are saying about Chris Mullin:

"He is not that quick, but he is *so* smart."

–Rick Adelman,
former NBA coach

"I've been around a lot of superstars who don't work nearly as hard as Chris."

–David Wood, teammate

"He has great court vision and some of the greatest hands I've ever seen."

–Don Nelson,
former Warriors head coach

"If I had to pick one guy to attempt the last shot with the game on the line, Mullin would by my choice."

—*Doug Collins,*
  Detroit Pistons head coach

"He's one of the best I've ever seen at taking a hit and finishing a shot."

—*Rod Higgins,*
  former Warriors assistant

"When God made basketball, he just carved out Chris Mullin and said, 'This is a basketball player.'"

—*Magic Johnson,*
  NBA legend

Career

Highlights

Chris Mullin ranks among the finest team players in basketball history. In high school, college, and the NBA, he has done whatever it takes to make his team better. At one time or another, Chris has led his team in every category—from steals to assists to rebounds. And he is one of the best pure shooters ever to step on a basketball court.

Chris was a two-time All-American at St. John's University.

Chris is a two-time Olympic gold medalist. He played for the United States at the 1984 games in Los Angeles, and he was a member of the famous Dream Team that won gold at the Barcelona games in 1992.

Chris celebrates
St. John's win that
sent them to the
Final Four in the 1985
NCAA tournament.

Chris led the
NBA in minutes
played during the
1990–91 and 1991–92
seasons.

Chris was voted Big East Player of the Year in 1984. He averaged 22.9 points and 4.0 assists per game in 1983–84.

Chris was honored as NCAA Player of the Year in 1985.

Chris has played in five NBA All-Star Games. In the 1992 contest, he hit six of seven shots and dished out three assists.

Chris made the All-NBA First Team in 1992, joining superstars Karl Malone, Clyde Drexler, David Robinson, and Michael Jordan.

Chris averaged more than 25 points per game for five straight seasons. Among active players, only Michael Jordan, Karl Malone, and Dominique Wilkins have equaled this achievement.

Reaching

In 1988, Chris Mullin began chatting with Warriors ball girl Francine Williams. They started talking about their families and their dreams for the future. One of her desires was to get a college education, but she could not afford the tuition. Soon, they became good friends. One day, Chris gave her some great news: he had decided to pay her college tuition. Francine enrolled at San Jose State University, becoming the first person in her family ever to go to college.

"It feels really good to help someone, and I try to do as much as I can. I work with the United Way, the American Heart Association, and the Discovery Museum. In the summer, I run a basketball camp for young kids, and we have a great time."

Chris has established the Chris Mullin Fund, which raises money for poor families and children.

Out

Golden State WARRIORS

SPALDING
Endorsed by the NBA

NBA STAY IN SCHOOL

THE CHRIS MULLIN FUND
FOR FAMILIES, CHILDREN AND YOUTH

17

Numbers

Name: Christopher Paul Mullin
Nickname: "Mully"
Born: July 30, 1963
Height: 6' 7"

Weight: 215 pounds
Uniform Number: 17
College: St. John's University

Chris has more career points than most of the players already enshrined in the Basketball Hall of Fame. In 1991, he became the first Warrior to start an All-Star Game since Rick Barry in 1978.

Year	Games	Shooting Percentage	Free Throw Percentage	Points	Points Per Game
1985-86	55	.463	.896	768	14.0
1986-87	82	.514	.825	1,242	15.1
1987-88	60	.508	.885	1,213	20.2
1988-89	82	.509	.892	2,176	26.5
1989-90	78	.536	.889	1,956	25.1
1990-91	82	.536	.884	2,107	25.7
1991-92	81	.524	.833	2,074	25.6
1992-93	46	.510	.810	1,191	25.9
1993-94	62	.472	.753	1,040	16.8
1994-95	25	.489	.879	476	19.0
1995-96	55	.499	.856	734	13.3
Totals	708	.512	.862	14,977	21.2

What If...

When I made the decision to be a basketball player, I worked as hard as I could to make that dream come true. The way I see it, you get as much out of life as you put into it. What if something had prevented me from playing ball? I would probably be working on Wall Street, maybe as a stockbroker or an analyst. I worked there during the summer when I was in school and found the stock market very exciting. I think I'd be good at it, too. Even though it would have been my second choice for a career, I still would have approached it with as much determination and focus as I have devoted to basketball."

Glossary

CUSTOMS INSPECTOR an officer who inspects people's luggage when they are traveling from one country to another to make sure that nobody carries illegal goods across a border

ANALYST a person who examines a situation and makes recommendations

CONSENSUS general agreement; popular opinion

STOCKBROKER one who handles the buying and selling of stocks, bonds, and shares in companies

TUITION money paid to attend a school or college

WALL STREET a street in New York City where the New York Stock Exchange is located; the stock market

ENSHRINED so highly respected as to be voted in to a Hall of Fame

INTERNATIONAL reaching beyond the boundaries of the United States

PRIORITY first in importance

RECRUITER one who tries to get people to join their team or organization

REGIMEN a regularly scheduled plan of activities or exercises

Index

About The Author

Mark Stewart grew up in New York City in the 1960s and 1970s— when the Mets, Jets, and Knicks all had championship teams. As a child, Mark read everything about sports he could lay his hands on. Today, he is one of the busiest sportswriters around. Since 1990, he has written close to 500 sports stories for kids, including profiles on more than 200 athletes, past and present. A graduate of Duke University, Mark served as senior editor of *Racquet*, a national tennis magazine, and was managing editor of *Super News*, a sporting goods industry newspaper. He is the author of every Grolier All-Pro Biography.